Find Me

A Play

Olwen Wymark

A SAMUEL FRENCH ACTING EDITION

SAMUEL FRENCH

FOUNDED 1830

SAMUELFRENCH.COM
SAMUELFRENCH-LONDON.CO.UK

FOR PRODUCTION ENQUIRIES

UNITED STATES AND CANADA
Info@SamuelFrench.com
1-866-598-8449

UNITED KINGDOM AND EUROPE
Theatre@SamuelFrench-London.co.uk
020-7255-4302

Each title is subject to availability from Samuel French, depending upon country of performance. Please be aware that FIND ME may not be licensed by Samuel French in your territory. Professional and amateur producers should contact the nearest Samuel French office or licensing partner to verify availability.

FIND ME

First performed at the Richmond Fringe Theatre at the
Orange Tree on October 21st 1977

Cast

Liz Crowther	Sharman Macdonald
Cherith Mellor	Cindy O'Callaghan
Auriol Smith	Andrew Branch
Robert East	Rio Fanning

Directed by Sam Walters

Subsequently performed at The Actors Theatre Louis-
ville Kentucky as a prize-winning new play in February
1979, and directed by Jon Jory

This play is dedicated to the real "Verity"

ACKNOWLEDGEMENTS

My most particular thanks to the parents of the girl who is called Verity in this play. The story of *Find Me* is true and the real Verity is at the time of writing in Rampton Prison. Her parents very generously gave all the information that was needed for the play and made themselves available for questions and discussion while it was being written.

My very grateful thanks to the students who worked with me on the play through improvisation and discussion while I was Gulbenkian Writer in Residence at Kingston Polytechnic in Surrey in 1977: Jenny Ashby, David Blenkinsop, Arina Brookes, Penny Dawes, Hilary Fowler, Anita Pearce, Carolyn Ryall, Nuala Scannell, Kathy Spooner, Jenny Swanson, Liz Taber and Philip Tong. Also thanks to their Technical Advisor, Andy Bridger-Wilkinson and very special thanks to their teacher Bernice Slynn whose original suggestion it was to write this play and who directed these students in *Find Me* both at Kingston Polytechnic and at the Edinburgh Festival in 1977.

PRODUCTION NOTE

This version of the play is based on the open stage production as played at the Orange Tree Theatre. The play was there performed by a cast of eight, five women and three men, all the parts being shared among them. The production was played without special costumes and with no props. In this text I have given the performers numbers to indicate where changes of role take place. Obviously more performers can be accommodated in the play but it is essential that the main parts change hands from scene to scene.

CHARACTERS

Verity I	Nurse
Verity II	Admissions Clerk
Verity III	Assistant Registrar
Verity IV	Doctor I
Verity V	Doctor II
Narrator	Miss Everitt, a social worker
Edward I	Dottie, a staff member
Edward II	Tom, a warden
Edward III	Valerie, a little old lady
Jean	Harry
Nicky	Geoff
Mark	Consultant Psychiatrist
Interviewer	Ted
Teacher	Dora
Mother I	Sister Moses
Mother II	Geriatric Patient I
Waitress	Geriatric Patient II
French Mother	Geriatric Patient III
French Father	Geriatric Patient IV
French Child	Miss Blake, physiotherapist
Neighbour I	
Neighbour II	Schoolchildren, Mothers, Voices

The action of the play takes place on a bare stage
There is one optional interval

Time—the present

FIND ME

A bare stage

The Lights come up on the five Veritys on a raised area upstage. The three Actors stand in the surrounding darkness

Narrator In November nineteen seventy-five, at the age of twenty, Verity Taylor was charged by the Police with damaging a chair by fire—value six pounds—in a locked ward of a mental hospital where she was a patient. She was remanded in custody to Holloway Prison for a period of three months. She was subsequently tried at Canterbury Crown Court and in February nineteen seventy-six an order was made for her admission to a maximum security hospital. On February the twenty-fourth, nineteen seventy-six, Verity Taylor was admitted to Broadmoor, from where she may not be discharged or transferred elsewhere without the permission of the Home Secretary.

Verity I Dear whoever you are, find me and have me as your beloved.

Verity II Find me. (*She leaves the lighted area*)

Verity III Find me. (*She leaves the lighted area*)

Verity IV Find me. (*She leaves the lighted area*)

Verity V Find me. (*She leaves the lighted area*)

The Light stays on Verity I, who remains throughout the following, kneeling and hugging herself in her arms. The Lights come up in another area on Verity II, who is waving hands, smiling, hopping, dancing, walking in a curious duck-like way

Edward I All right, Verity, move out of the way now. I want to take some pictures of Mummy and the boys.

Verity II No no, I'm on the movies. I'm on the movies! (*She continues waving, smiling, etc.*)

Nicky (Verity III) I want a go, Dad. Take my picture. It isn't fair! Mark, tell her! Tell her it's my turn, Mark.

Mark (Edward III) Get out of the way Verity. Anyone would think you were six instead of sixteen. Just get out of the way!

Verity II No! Take some more of me, Dad.

Edward II Now now, Verity. Let Nicholas and Mark have a turn. I want to take the whole family.

Jean (Verity IV) Verity, stop being so silly. Do as Daddy says.

Mark Get out of the way, Verity!

Nicky It isn't fair.

Edward III Behave yourself, Verity. You've had your turn.

Jean (Verity V) Verity, stop being so silly. Do as Daddy says.

Edward I Be a good girl, Verity.

All,
except Veritys } (*one after another*) Be a good girl, Verity.
I and II

Verity II (*very loudly*) No! (*She freezes. Then kneels in the posture of Verity I*)

Nicky I think it is a great pity about my sister's illness. I hardly ever see her nowadays. I might say I hardly knew her. She was sent away as an in-patient when I was only a few months old. Last year when I was ten she was sent up to Broadmoor which was brought on by an accident at the mental hospital. She was always very kind to me. I think upon this as a tragedy about my sister and when I think of it I sometimes cannot stop myself from crying.

Verity I Find me.
Verity II Find me.

The Lights go out on Veritys I and II and come up on the Interviewer and Edward III

Interviewer The birth was normal?

Edward Yes, except that she was a little premature. Her mother wasn't allowed to have her with her for the first week.

Interviewer And she's now nine years old—is that correct?

Edward Yes.

Interviewer When did you first notice symptoms of abnormality in Verity?

Edward (*distressed*) We weren't thinking about "symptoms". We've never considered her to be abnormal. She's just . . .

Interviewer (*not unkindly*) Your doctor is asking us to see her here at the Child Guidance Clinic. In his report he speaks of bizarre and anti-social behaviour.

Edward (*helplessly*) She's a difficult child.

Interviewer Has she always been difficult? What was she like as a small infant?

Edward (*sadly*) She never smiled. (*Pause*) When she looked at you it seemed sometimes as if she didn't really see you.

Interviewer Not affectionate? Responsive? Warm?

Edward No—no, not really.

Interviewer At what age did she begin to walk?

Edward Well, a little late. She was about two. The thing was she didn't seem to have any—sense of territory.

Interviewer Sense of territory?

Edward Any homing instinct. It was as if she had no idea where she belonged. We had to watch her all the time. She'd just wander off, you see.

Interviewer Did you find that she became more affectionate as she grew older?

Edward Oh yes, she . . . (*He breaks off*) Well, she was always a little—distant. She doesn't like to be touched. Even as a toddler she wouldn't sit in your lap, let you cuddle her. She's a very private little person. Introverted, I've always said.

Interviewer Does she talk?

Edward Oh, she talks very well—though she does get a little muddled up sometimes. It can be a bit difficult to get through to her. But then she's quite an emotional girl. There are times when she'll just sit—you know —silent. Won't talk to anyone. Other times shen she gets excited there's no stopping her. Moody, we think.

Interviewer Is her behaviour ever aggressive?

Edward Well yes, there are tantrums sometimes. She'll flare up very suddenly. Shout, run about the house slamming doors—that sort of thing. Usually at night. The nights have always been—hard. She cried every night until she was a year old—nearly all night long. There didn't seem any way to comfort her. (*Hastily*) Of course she's much better now. Quite often we'll have whole nights without any trouble.

Interviewer Has she persisted in wandering off from home?

Edward Yes, I'm afraid that she has. She's always being brought back by strangers—on one or two occasions by the police. Just silly tomboyish things, really. Trespass, a bit of minor vandalism. Nothing serious. (*With an attempt at a laugh*) Once she let some pigs loose on a farm near us.

Interviewer Did you ever punish her?

Edward At first we did, of course. Just a smack. Nothing very . . . It was disastrous. She seemed to go absolutely wild, screaming, throwing herself about. Or else she'd just become rigid and silent. Sometimes for hours. We decided that any kind of physical punishment was wrong for Verity. She's an incredibly sensitive child.

Interviewer I see. You never considered getting help with Verity before, Mr Taylor?

Edward No. We didn't think anything was seriously wrong, you see. You get used to things don't you. We just thought she was going through some funny phases. She was very different from her brother, Mark. He's three years older—but no two children are alike. Then last year our doctor discovered that Verity had a mild epileptic condition. She's on drugs for that now. We thought that probably explained why she was so . . . We hoped she'd settle down.

Interviewer And she hasn't.

Edward No. If anything she's . . . (*With a kind of eagerness*) She's an intelligent child, you know. She's not stupid. She can be very imaginative, very witty. They're quite pleased with her progress at her primary school.

Interviewer She plays with other children? Has friends?

Edward No—no—she usually plays alone. She doesn't seem to get on a wavelength with other children somehow. We've noticed that she veers between being a little too—er—high-spirited or closed up in a funny way. You get children like that, don't you, who are just solitary by nature. She always seems so much happier playing in her own little private world.

Verity III comes on into a lighted area and kneels on the floor

When she was very small she used to play for hours on end with a village she built out of blocks.

Verity III (*building her village, very concentrated*) There's the school—and the church—and here's all the houses—and here's the park—and this is the castle. (*She sits back on her heels and looks at it*) It's my village. It's tiny tiny tiny, and it's all mine. I'm big and I look after all the people. (*She stretches her arms out over the village. Crooning*) I'll take care of you. I'll take care of you. (*She starts building again*) I'll make a lovely big swimming pool—and here's where the horses live. There's a hundred horses and if they want to they can gallop through the whole village. Gallop gallop gallop down the streets, and jump over the hedges and in the gardens and . . .

Edward II enters

Edward II Hello, Verity. What's that you're making?

Verity is immediately silent and stiff

Verity (*sharply*) Be careful. You'll step on it.
Edward I won't. I won't. I'll be careful. What is it?
Verity (*still warily*) It's my village.
Edward Oh, it's very nice. Clever girl.
Verity This is my castle. (*She looks at him sideways*) I'm inside it.
Edward Are you?
Verity Yes. And nobody else can get in.
Edward Well well!
Verity It's all locked up and safe and they can't get in.

Jean (Verity IV) comes in

Jean Hello, darling. You're back. (*She moves to Edward*)
Verity Look out!
Jean What?
Verity You're knocking it over!
Jean (*good-naturedly*) Well honestly, Verity, you've taken up nearly the whole floor. Look, you'll have to move it now anyway. We've going to have tea in here. (*She stoops to pick up a block*)
Verity (*fiercely*) Don't touch that!
Edward (*with a warning look to Jean*) We won't touch any of it, Verity. You put it away yourself.
Verity I don't want to put it away. I want to play with it.
Jean You can play with it later.
Verity I don't want later. I want now!
Jean We're going to have tea.
Verity I don't care! Now now now! I want my village now!
Jean Stop shouting like that and do as you're told.
Verity (*insolently*) What? What? What did you say? I'm deaf. I can't hear you. I'm deaf. I'm deaf.
Jean (*beginning to lose control*) I said to do as I tell you.
Edward Jean—don't.

Verity (*violently knocking over some of the village*) You tell me! You tell me! Mine! It isn't yours. I'll break it. (*Rising and kicking the blocks*) I'm smashing it. You can't have it!
Edward Verity—stop!

Verity does stop, and pushes past her mother as she goes out

Verity They're all dead now. They're killed. That's what you wanted. You wanted them killed.

Jean and Edward look at each other in silence for a moment

Jean (*starting uncertainly after Verity*) I'll go and talk to her.
Edward (*starting to pick up the blocks*) I should leave her. Let her simmer down.
Jean But Edward, she shouldn't be allowed to . . . Surely we mustn't let her behave like that. Why does she do it? I don't understand.
Edward (*busy, not looking at her*) All children have little temper tantrums. It's nothing—out of the way. I'll speak to her later.
Jean She doesn't do it to you. You don't know what she's like. Little temper tantrums! She torments me, Edward. Last week one night when you were away she burst into the bedroom about three o'clock in the morning with the radio turned up full blast. I made her turn it off and then she started dancing and stamping around the room and butting her head against the bed pretending to be a car. I tried to take her into bed with me but she wouldn't let me touch her. I took her back to her bedroom time and time again but the moment I dropped off she'd come rushing back in again. There was nothing I could do. She just went on and on.
Edward Why didn't you tell me?
Jean Because all I ever seem to do is complain to you about her. Other mothers cope. I feel so inadequate. Nothing seems to satisfy her. I can't seem to do anything right. I can't bear it. Sometimes I think I'll go mad. Last week when that happened I actually wanted to get up and run out of the house into the night. To get away from her. Escape from my own child. Sometimes I feel as though she's punishing me for something. It's as if she's taking some kind of revenge. But why? Why?
Edward You're tired. Come on, I'll make you a cup of tea. You wait until she goes to school. It'll make all the difference.
Jean Do you think so?
Edward Course it will. When she comes up against kids her own age. You'll see.

Edward and Jean go off

The Lights fade, and come up on a Teacher reading a report

Teacher Verity Taylor, Class Two. Average age of class nine years and six months. End of term report: English: composition thirty-six out of fifty, comprehension seventy-two out of one hundred, grammar fifty-two out of one hundred, spelling and dictation forty-five out of fifty, science thirty out of forty, art, good, writing fair, reading good, P.T. and games, very good. Verity has tried very hard in class to the best of her ability and has made progress. She is still unreliable in her social behaviour out of class, in lunch hours etc., but has been very helpful as an early morning monitor. (*He turns and calls*) Come along, Class Two. Hurry up.

The Lights fade, then come up on the downstage area

Jean (Verity V) enters with an umbrella. Another Mother enters, with a newspaper over her head

Mother I Isn't it awful.
Jean Awful. Do share my umbrella.
Mother I Oh ta. That is kind. Come on so sudden, didn't it? And I sent my Robert this morning without his wellies.
Jean Me too. I brought Verity's with me. She insisted on wearing an old pair of plimsolls this morning.
Mother I Aren't they daft—children.
Jean (*after a brief pause*) Yes.

Mother II enters with an umbrella

Mother II (*to Mother I*) Hello. You well? Rotten old day isn't it?
Mother I Terrible. And I always get here early. Never seem to get it right. (*To Jean*) I'd be drowned if it wasn't for you.
Jean I expect they'd let us wait inside if we asked.
Mother II Oh I don't know so much. The headmistress is that fussy.
Jean Isn't it silly—I'm just as scared of headmistresses now as when I was at school myself.
Mother I Headmistresses and policemen. (*She laughs*)
Mother II Wasn't their nativity play lovely this year.
Mother I Lovely. That teacher, Miss Wright, she's ever so clever with the costumes.
Mother II And didn't they sing beautifully! Our Michael was an angel. Some angel!
Mother I You never get fed up with it do you? Year after year always the same but I do enjoy it.
Mother II (*to Jean*) Was yours in it this year?
Jean No. No, she wasn't very well.
Mother II So much flu about, isn't there.
Jean Yes.

The Lights fade, then come up on the Teacher. The Children—including the former Edward, Jean and Verity—sit as in class. Verity IV sits a little apart

Teacher Right. What are the primary colours of light?

Several hands go up

Tracy.
A Child Red, sir.

Teacher Yes, good. (*To another*) Keith?
Another Child Blue.
Teacher That's right. And . . .
A third Child (*waving a hand wildly*) Yellow, sir.
Teacher No, not yellow.

More hands go up—not Verity's

What about you, Verity? Do you know?

Verity nods

Well? Tell us.
Verity Green.
Teacher Green of course. Good. You collect the pencils for me, will you?
And don't forget to bring your packed lunches tomorrow everyone. For
the British Museum outing. There's the bell. Off you go then.

*All the Children except Verity scramble out, grabbing coats and things,
punching one another, shouting, etc., and run into the playground, where the
Mothers are waiting. Verity, unnoticed by the Teacher, stands holding up
the pencils*

*The Mothers and Children talk as the Mothers button up coats, asking
about books, etc.*

Oh. Thank you, Verity. (*She takes them*) Run along now.

*The Mothers and Children continue talking, buttoning up coats, asking about
books, etc.*

Jean Verity!

Verity does not look up

Verity, I'm over here.

Verity looks up

Verity (*very loudly*) Hullo, you old cow!

The Mothers look up and then look away. Jean hurries to Verity

Jean I've brought your wellingtons.
Verity Oh good. I'll have a drink out of them. (*She grabs one of the boots
and scoops up water from a puddle. Stamping about in the puddle, she
pretends to drink*) Ooooh lovely! Champagne!
Jean Don't be silly, Verity. Put them on. Here I'll help you.

Verity runs away from her. Jean chases her: she is very embarrassed

A Child That's Verity. We call her the mad woman that sits on the wall.
Mother I Ssssshhhh!
A Child She's crazy. Nobody likes her.
Mother II (*to Mother I*) I've heard about her. She ought to be in a special
school really.
Mother I It's a shame. Her poor mother.

Verity (*holding out the boot to Jean*) Want a sip? Well you can't have it! (*She rushes over to Mother II and proffers boot*) Do you want a drink of champagne?
Mother II (*to her child*) Come along, Michael, quickly now.

The Mothers get their Children together and go off

Mother I turns back

Mother I (*to Jean*) Cheeribye.

Mother I goes

Jean waves rather forlornly. Then she and Verity are left alone at some distance from each other in the empty playground

Jean Verity, I'm going now.
Verity I'll go first. See if you can catch me. (*She laughs*) You can't catch me.

Verity runs off

Jean (*following, distraught*) Verity! Wait—Verity!

Jean goes

The Lights come up on Mark sitting down stage, dressed in school blazer. He gets up and stands with his arms folded, scuffing one foot on the floor, or perhaps moving about in a frustrated way

Mark I wish I didn't have to live at home. You never know what she's going to do next. I can't bring my friends to our house. I wouldn't. I don't want them to know what she's like. When she watches something she likes on TV she goes (*exaggeratedly he rubs and claps his hands together, bobbing up and down*). And if she can't get what she wants she goes around making an awful face and saying "Neetz! Neetz! Neetz!" She does that in the shops sometimes when Mum won't buy her something she wants. Everybody staring . . . And sometimes at night she'll go all over the house banging in and out of all our rooms. Dad's had to put locks on all the inside doors in the house. When she gets like that you just have to lock her out to get a bit of peace. And she never has meals with us because all she does is jump around and grab things. She won't sit down and eat properly so she has to eat by herself. She goes to the Child Guidance but it doesn't do any good. I don't know . . . (*Pause. Very frustrated*) And there's nobody I can tell about it. Nobody to talk to. Mum would just get upset. Cry maybe. And Dad would say to me, "Come along Mark old chap. Remember it's not easy for Verity." Well it's not easy for me either! (*Pause*) We went on a camping holiday to France last summer. She spoiled everything. We went out one night to a restaurant . . .

Edward II, Verity III as Jean and Verity II come on

Edward . . . for a treat. You'd like that wouldn't you, Verity?
Verity Oh yes. *Mais oui!* That's right, isn't it, Dad?

Edward (*laughing*) That's right. *Mais oui.*
Verity Oh Mum, can I get dressed up? I wish I'd brought my party dress.
  I love getting dressed up. I want to look pretty to go to the restaurant.
Jean (*smiling, hugging her*) You do look pretty. You look very pretty.
Edward Come on then everyone. Come along Mark.

Jean, Edward and Verity go off, Mark dawdling behind

The Lights come up on a Waitress preparing tables. A very proper French family come in, Mother, Father, Child. They bring on chairs. The Waitress sets other chairs

Waitress *Bon soir, Madame, M'sieur, bon soir mon enfant. Assayez vous, je vous en prie. Assayez vous.*

They sit, and she takes their order

The Taylor family come in

The Waitress smiles at them

  (*In bad English*) Good evening. Please to take seats.
Verity (*going to her, excitedly*) *Je comprends! Je comprends! Bon soir.*
Jean Sit down, Verity.

Verity cranes to look at the other table

Verity They've got a little girl. Hullo *enfant!*
Mark (*in an angry whisper*) Sit down!

The Waitress comes over to their table, greets them

Edward Sit here by me, Verity. We're going to order now.

Verity sits and puts the menu on her head

Jean Verity, please . . .

Verity takes the menu off her head and looks at it

Verity Oh look. Poison! They give you poison here. (*She shows the menu to the waitress*) Do you serve poison?
Waitress *Poisson, Mam'selle?* Some fish?
Jean I'll have melon to start, Edward.
Mark Me too.
Verity (*laughing*) Melly belly smelly telly!
Mark (*kicking at her under the table*) Oh shut up.

The French family studiously avoid all this

Edward I'll have soup. You'd like soup, wouldn't you, Verity?
Waitress *Deux soupes* and *deux melons M'sieu?* (*She holds up two fingers*)
Verity Oh rude! Look what she's doing, Dad. (*She stabs her two fingers up in the air*) *Deux et deux*, Dad!
Jean Stop, Verity. Don't be silly, dear.

The Waitress goes and gets the first course for the French family and serves them. They begin to eat, highly stylized, rather ritualistic. Verity picks up everyone's napkins and chucks them into their laps

Verity Put your napkins in your laps. That's what's polite. Has the *enfant* got her napkin in her lap? (*She dances over to the other table*) Oh good! *Bon! Bon!*

Edward Verity, come back here!

Verity (*dancing back*) Here I am, Dad. Did you miss me? (*She sits clumsily*) Ooooops. *Garçon!* I've dropped my spoon. *Garçon!*

The Waitress comes over to their table with a tray

(*Very haughtily*) Hey you!

She points to the floor. The Waitress puts down the tray, picks up the spoon and gives Verity a clean one from the tray

Merci beaucoup. Merci beaucoup. (*She looks at the tray. Very loudly*) *Ici la* fucking soup. (*She laughs*) *Ici la* fucking soup!

Jean pushes back her chair

Mark It's O.K., Mum. Don't worry.

Edward How about some wine? For a special treat. (*He orders wine from the Waitress*)

Verity Mum'll get drunk. She'll get drunk. (*She gets up and does a drunk walk staggering over to the other table*) Regardez! Regardez! I'm drunk!

Edward Verity! Come here at once.

Verity comes back and sits but swivels round in her chair to watch the French family as they eat, carefully oblivious of her

Verity Look at them. They're daft. (*She mimics the way they are eating in an exaggerated way*)

The little French girl watches, fascinated. Her family efficiently shift their places so that the child cannot see Verity. Verity makes a loud raspberry at them and holds two fingers up

Deux et deux to you too!

Jean (*getting up*) I can't bear this.

Mark (*half getting up*) Sit down, Mum. Please sit down. Everybody in the place is looking at us.

Jean (*pained and proud*) Not because of me. I'm going.

Jean goes out and Mark follows her

Mark (*quietly and venomously to Verity, as he goes*) I hate you!

Mark goes

Edward Come along, Verity. We're going now. (*He puts money on the table*)

Verity But I haven't finished. I don't want to go. (*She starts greedily eating soup*)

Edward (*angrily, but controlled*) Now! (*He gets her to her feet*)

Waitress (*coming over*) M'sieu, I have open the wine already. It is necessary that you pay for the wine.

Edward Oh yes. Of course. Yes. (*He takes out more money and hands it over*) I'm sorry—pardon—I'm very sorry. (*He takes Verity by the hand and starts to pull her out*)

Verity (*to the Waitress*) Out of the way, please. My father wishes to go forward. (*She turns and shouts at French family*) He's not my real father. I'm a bastard. They're going to take me back and drown me! They're going to put me in a bucket and drown me!

Laughing, Verity allows herself to be dragged out

With one accord the French family look off in the direction Verity and Edward went. They freeze, then they pick up the chairs, the Waitress helping, and pile them up C. *There is the sound of children's voices off, singing "Remember, Remember, the Fifth of November"*

French Mother (now Neighbour) What about this old chair, Jean? Does that go on the bonfire too?

Verity, Jean and Edward come back on as Neighbour and Children and help with bonfire

French Child (now Jean) Oh yes, put it on. It's falling apart anyway.

French Dad (now Child) This is bigger than last year's bonfire, isn't it, Mrs Taylor?

Jean (*laughing*) Lot's bigger, Sammy.

Waitress (now Verity) And we've got millions and millions of bangers and rockets and catherine wheels and roman candles . . . (*She runs about excitedly*) Zzzzzzzzzz—bang!

Jean Verity, not so noisy—you'll wake the baby.

Verity He doesn't get to see the fireworks. He's too little. He has to stay in bed and miss the party. Ha, ha, ha. Silly Nicky has to stay in bed. Silly Nicky—silly Nicky. (*She sings and dances about*)

Neighbour I How is the baby, Jean? Oh God, how I remember those middle-of-the-night feeds.

Jean He's as good as gold. He's been sleeping right through for the last fortnight. Isn't that good for three months.

Neighbour I Marvellous. Lucky you.

Neighbour II (*coming over, nodding towards Verity who is still singing and dancing about*) She's in good spirits tonight, eh?

Jean She loves fireworks. She's been looking forward to this for weeks.

Neighbour I She seems fine, Jean. She came over and helped me do some weeding yesterday. We had a lovely chat.

Jean She's liking the new school. Especially the swimming. She's got so good at swimming we've been amazed.

Mark from the previous scene—now Edward—comes on

Edward Everybody got a drink? Who'd like a drink? (*He goes round pouring*)

Verity I haven't. I haven't. I want a drink, Dad. Can I have some wine?
I want some wine.

Edward What, at eleven years old? I'd get arrested. You can have a Coke
—and get some for the other children.

*Verity gets Cokes for her and other Children, who are all a bit wary of her
but grab the Cokes*

Child I Where's Mark? Why isn't he at the party?

Verity He's on School Journey. I'm the only child, aren't I, Dad? Mum!
Mum! I'm the only child.

Jean (*laughing*) Yes.

Edward Well, you are for tonight, Verity.

Verity I'm the king of the castle and you're the dirty rascal!
I'm the king of the castle and you're the dirty rascal!

Verity pushes one of the Children and knocks her over. Child cries

Jean Verity! Don't be so rough.

Verity (*to the Child, puzzled*) What are you crying for? We're having a
party.

Neighbour I Get up, Lucy, and don't be such a baby. Verity didn't mean
to hurt you.

Edward (*glancing gratefully at her*) Here, Lucy, have some crisps.

The Child is snufflingly pacified

Child II When are we going to have the fireworks? Can we have the
fireworks now?

Child III And the bonfire! Let's light the bonfire!

Verity Yes! Yes! Yes, yes, yes! Fireworks, fireworks! Bonfire, bonfire!

Neighbour II (*laughing*) It's not dark yet. We have to wait till it's dark for
the bonfire.

Edward Sausages and baked potatoes first, eh?

Child II Yuk. I hate sausages. Yuk.

Neighbour I (*clouting him*) Don't be rude or you'll go home to bed, you
hear me?

Child II Oh, Mum . . .

Jean There's bacon rolls, too. But the potatoes aren't quite done yet.
Only a few minutes more.

Verity Not potatoes! Bonfire! Now! Now! Fireworks! Bonfire! Now!
Now!

Edward (*going to Verity*) Calm down, chicken. I tell you what. Why don't
you recite your poem for all of us—the one you wrote at school last
week. (*To the others, proudly*) She's learned it by heart.

Neighbour II Oh yes. Come on, Verity, let's hear it.

Child III I bet she didn't write it herself. Verity can't write poems.

Verity (*upset*) I did. I did. It's my poem. I wrote it in my book myself.

Neighbour I Course she did. I bet it's very good. Go on, Verity.

*The Lights begin to fade on the stage to a kind of glow and Verity moves a
little apart from the others, who are left in half darkness*

Verity Listen to the old mill creek
The rain falls on to old leaves
Silent ears hear. Suddenly
The silence is broken by someone
Letting off a banger.

Swishing through golden leaves
An owl hoots.
A vole rushes to his home.
The whispering dawn comes near
As evening runs out of time.

A blue moon is out
The sky is dark
As I walk slowly through the wood
Crunch crack swish the leaves under my feet
Make a colourful noise.

There is a brief silence. Then, from the half-dark, people say in quiet voices
"Lovely, Verity", "Beautiful", "What a lovely poem Verity", etc., and they
all clap. Verity stands smiling

Jean Come on, everyone, time for food!
Edward And while we're eating I'll start the fireworks.
Verity Oh yes, Dad! Oh yes!
Children Hooray! Hooray!
Edward (*loudly*) And light the fire.
Others (*softly in unison, rising in sound*) Light the fire! Light the fire!
Light the fire!

A red spot flickers on the bonfire. Verity throws her arms out in joy. There
is a sound of rockets and fireworks as she dances round the fire

Verity (*exalted*) The fire! The fire! The beautiful fire! (*She freezes with*
her arms up)

The flicker spot goes out

The Teacher comes on followed by the others

Teacher Come along, Class Three. Get the chairs and set them up by the
swimming-pool for our visitors.

Now everyone but the Teacher is a child. They clear the chairs from the
stage

Now remember. The swimming-gala starts at two o'clock sharp. All
those taking part this afternoon report to me at ten minutes to two in
your bathing costumes in the changing-room. And remember what I
told you. Any child not bringing a bathing-cap will not be allowed to
swim in the gala. Don't forget.

The Teacher goes off. The five Veritys come on. They begin to move about
in the central area, doing different swimming-strokes with their arms

Verity I I love to swim. I'm happy swimming. I'm free. I'm the best swimmer in my class. Miss said so. She said, "Verity you're the best in the class". She did. I'm the best in the school. I'm the best in England. I'm the best in the world. I'm the best in the whole universe. You're safe in the water. Safe as safe.

Verity II When I grow up I'm going to be an Olympics Champion. Verity Taylor, gold medallist. I'll be on television and I'll make a speech and everyone'll cheer and they'll clap and clap and all the little children will ask me for my autograph. And I'll meet the Queen. And the sun will be shining on the water and on my gold medal and on her gold crown and she'll shake my hand. She'll love me. Everybody will love me.

Verity III One day I'll swim the English Channel. On and on and on I'll go until I get to France. I'll be strong and I won't be scared of the waves or the sharks. And my dad'll be in the boat beside me feeding me sandwiches and lemonade. He'll say, "Come on, Verity. You can do it." And I will. I'll go on and on and on.

Verity IV When I swim in the pool the water is blue and green and silver. It's soft and I feel like I'm flying. I'm a flying fish. I'm a seagull. Floating, drifting, flying, swishing. Lovely swimming, Lovely water. I kick my feet as I go along and the splashing says, "Verity, Verity, Verity, Verity".

Verity V When I'm in bed at night I dream about swimming. I'm swimming in the sea and I'm riding in the foam of the waves and I wave at all the people in the boats and they wave back. Sometimes I dream I'm swimming all by myself in a lake high up in the mountains. I'm all alone except for the birds and the fishes. Don't be afraid of the snakes. They're only water snakes. They won't hurt you. It's my lake. Verity Lake in the Verity Mountains.

Verity I Today I'll win all the prizes in the swimming gala.

Verity II My mum and dad'll be watching and they'll be proud as proud.

Verity III Mark and Nicky'll wish they were me.

Verity IV At the end I'll just stand there smiling.

Verity V The winner! The winner! Verity Taylor the winner!

The Lights snap to Black-out

Teacher (*out of darkness*) What's your name, girl?

Verity Verity Taylor, Miss.

Teacher Where's your swimming-cap?

Verity I haven't got it.

Teacher Well, run and fetch it.

Verity (*panicky*) I left it at home. I forgot it.

Teacher (*briskly*) No-one without a cap is allowed to swim. It's the rules. You can't swim in the gala this afternoon, Verity.

Verity (*loudly, in despair*) No! No! No!

The Lights come up on Verity standing utterly rigid and silent, catatonic. Edward, Jean and Mark approach her, stopping a few feet away

Edward Don't be upset, Verity. There, there, darling. It's not the end of the world.

Jean There'll be another swimming-gala next year. You'll be able to swim in that one.

Mark (*not meaning to be unkind*) You're stupid, Verity. It was your own fault. There's no point blaming anybody.

Jean Don't tease her, Mark.

Edward You'll have forgotten about it by morning.

Mark Well, say something why don't you.

They move toward her, Jean and Edward with their arms outstretched

Verity (*throwing out her arms to stop them. Ferociously*) Don't touch me!

Verity backs away from them and then rushes off, shouting

Don't touch me! Leave me alone. Don't touch me! No! No! No! Neetz! Neetz! Neetz!

Black-out. In the darkness we hear banging and thumping and Verity's voice howling, growling and screaming out incoherent words. The voices of Edward, Mark and Jean come from different places on the stage

Jean Verity, where are you? What are you doing? Oh Edward, Edward! She's torn up all my photographs and my letters. Look, look—she's torn up everything. Oh God, Edward, stop her. What's she doing?

Edward I can't. She's locked herself in the bathroom.

There is a sound of pounding on a door

Verity, come out! Come out!

There is the sound of rushing water as Verity goes on shouting

Mark Dad, there's water coming out from under the door. She's flooding the bathroom. She'll flood the whole house.

Edward Verity, come out! Stop that! Come out of there!

Jean (*crying*) Oh my God, my God, my God.

Mark Stop her, Dad. I'm afraid.

Verity (*in a huge voice*) Look out! Get out of my way!

The Lights come up on Verity IV all alone on the stage. She is wearing a bizarre collection of clothes, and a wig with half the hair cut off it. She has make-up all over her face like a wild mask of warpaint

Look out! Can't you see? I'm the bomb! I'm the atom bomb! Don't touch me. Don't come near me! I'll blow you all up! (*She runs across the stage and through the auditorium and out screaming and shouting*) Don't touch me! Get out of my way! I'm the bomb. I'll blow you up! Look out! Look out!

Verity exits through the auditorium

The interval would come at this point if a break were planned

OPTIONAL INTERVAL

The stage is bare. Edward, Jean and Verity II stand in a little group in the middle. Verity II is completely blank and seems quite unaware of her parents' presence. She has a scarf tied over her head. On the raised area upstage sits Verity I as at the beginning, hugging herself in her own arms and kneeling

A Nurse comes on to the stage and walks briskly across, passing the Taylor family

Edward Excuse me.
Nurse Yes?
Edward We were told to wait in here but we . . .
Nurse Who did you want to see?
Jean We've brought our daughter to be—to be . . .
Edward Admitted. (*He clears his throat*) As a patient.
Verity I Dear Mum and Dad, I hope you're all right. If you get a map you can look up Broadmoor and then you will know where this place is. Perhaps you could write to me because I get very lonely here.
Nurse Who sent you in here?
Edward The porter at reception.
Jean We've been waiting nearly half-an-hour.
Nurse I'm sorry. We're very understaffed today, I'm afraid. It's the bank holiday.
Edward Yes.
Nurse He should have sent you straight to Admissions. If you'll just come this way. (*She starts to walk away*)

Edward and Jean both put a hand on Verity II's shoulders to bring her along. Swiftly and without looking at them she ducks out from under their hands and takes a step back. They look helplessly at the Nurse. She goes over to Verity and efficiently takes her hand. Verity neither resists nor looks at her

Come along, dear. Come with me. (*They start to walk and the others follow*) And what's your name, eh?

Verity II turns her head round suddenly and stares very intently into the Nurse's face. She says nothing

Never mind. I expect you'll tell me later.
Jean Verity. Her name's Verity.
Nurse That's a pretty name. Just along here.

The Admissions Clerk comes on in one corner of the stage carrying a chair, sits, starts to write

The Nurse brings the group up

New patient.
Clerk I'll be with you in a moment.
Nurse (*to the Taylors*) All right?
Edward Yes. Thank you.
Nurse (*going off*) Not at all. Bye-bye Verity.

There is no response from Verity II

The Nurse goes

Verity I There's a ward in this place called Katherine Ward. You go there if you do something bad. They sent me there because I ripped up some lino. It's cold in there.

Clerk (*looking up*) Name?

Edward Taylor. E. J. Taylor.

Clerk Name of patient?

Jean Verity Rose.

Clerk Age?

Edward Eleven years and—five months.

Clerk Date of birth?

Jean February the thirteenth, nineteen fifty-five.

Clerk Name and address of G.P.?

Edward Well, we . . .

Clerk You do have a letter from your doctor, do you?

Jean He's away. For the bank holiday. We had to find another doctor. (*Pause*) They all seemed to be away. It took such a long time . . .

Edward But we do have a doctor's letter, yes.

Clerk I think you'd better see the Assistant Registrar if the letter isn't from your own doctor. Just down that corridor and straight along to the end.

They turn to go. This time Edward carefully takes Verity II's hand. She does not resist and continues to be quite unaware of what is going on

The Assistant Registrar enters with a chair and sits

Jean, Edward and Verity II walk towards him

Verity I Some of the ones here have to sit with no clothes on in a small room. They just sit. Sometimes they throw themselves about.

Registrar Name?

Edward Taylor. E. J. Taylor.

Registrar Patient's name?

Edward Verity Rose.

Registrar Age?

Edward Eleven years and five months.

Registrar Date of birth?

Edward February the thirteenth, nineteen fifty-five.

Registrar Has your daughter been a patient here in the past?

Edward No.

Registrar Or in any other mental hospital?

Jean (*too loudly*) No! (*Awkwardly*) No, she hasn't.

Jean puts an arm round Verity's shoulders. Again Verity II swiftly ducks away, not looking at her

Registrar May I see your doctor's letter?

Edward (*handing it to him*) It isn't actually from our own doctor. He was away.

Jean (*softly, looking into Verity II's blank face*) Verity?

Verity I Oh God high in your heaven, please come and reveal for me. I need you now. Our father our father our father hold me in your hand. It's dark.

Registrar (*reading the letter*) "—severe anti-social behaviour culminating in actions that appear to me to justify hospitalization." Could you give me some details? When did this happen?

Edward Yesterday afternoon and evening. She broke three windows and locked herself into the bathroom and flooded it. She cut off a lot of her hair and she tore up a whole box full of letters and photographs. Just destroyed them utterly and threw them all over the room. Then she got herself dressed up in all sorts of strange clothes and ran out of the house.

Jean We couldn't stop her. She ran so fast. She was screaming and shouting and waving her arms about. We were terrified.

Edward She was missing for seven hours. We went out with friends looking everywhere for her. Then someone saw her knocking over dustbins outside her school and spreading the rubbish over the pavement.

Jean (*sadly*) In the dark.

They both look at Verity II, who is totally oblivious

Edward (*continuing with an effort*) They called the police. We'd notified them already of course but—(*pause*)—the police know Verity. They telephoned us. When we got her home she wouldn't speak to us or look at us. She went straight into the kitchen and opened a tin of sardines and covered them in jam. She ate them out of the tin with her fingers.

Jean She wouldn't go to bed. She lay on the floor under the kitchen table all night. When we—when we tried to touch her she kicked and—bit us.

Registrar Hmmmm—yes—yes—I see. There is a history of erratic behaviour?

Edward Yes.

Registrar And no previous psychiatric treatment?

Jean She's been attending the Child Guidance Clinic since she was nine.

Registrar And there have been specific epileptic features?

Edward Yes, she's been on medication for that for over three years now.

Registrar Well now, I think perhaps the best thing is if you go along and see one of our psychiatric staff before we go ahead with Admission. Third corridor on the left and up the stairs. (*He hands back the letter*) If you'll take this to the doctor . . .

Jean, Edward and Verity II walk across the stage

Doctor enters, carrying a chair, and sits

They stand in front of him

Verity I Sometimes I feel afraid that I will get lost in the dark maze of corridors here.

Doctor Sorry to keep you waiting so long. Your name is . . .

Edward Taylor. E. J. Taylor. (*He hands him the letter*)

Doctor And your daughter's name?

Edward Verity Rose.

Doctor And her age is . . .

Jean Eleven years and five months. She was born on February the thirteenth, nineteen fifty-five.

Doctor Has Verity had previous hospital treatment?

Edward No.

Doctor (*reading the letter*) "—to justify hospitalization." Can you tell me what happened?

Jean (*a little desperately*) They've asked us all this before.

Doctor Just for the records.

Edward (*rapidly*) She broke some windows. She cut off a lot of her hair and she flooded the bathroom. She destroyed a box of letters and photographs and she ran away from home dressed in bizarre clothes and screaming. The police brought her back seven hours later.

Doctor I see. Yes. And how are you feeling now, Verity?

Verity II gives no response at all.

Jean She hasn't spoken at all since last night.

Doctor Ah. And she's been on drugs for epileptic symptoms for how long?

Edward Three years.

Doctor No previous psychiatric treatment?

Edward She's been going to the Child Guidance Clinic.

Doctor I'd like you to take Verity along to see one of my colleagues who's on the staff for the children's ward. Room One B. You may have to wait a little I'm afraid. It's the bank holiday, you see. Just down the corridor and to the left.

A second Doctor comes on bringing a chair and sits

Verity I I have a fear of being alone in a small room.

Verity II moves c. *Jean and Edward stand together downstage. The following is very quick*

Registrar Date of birth?

Edward February the thirteenth, nineteen fifty-five.

Doctor II What exactly did she do?

Jean Cut off her hair.

Edward Screaming and waving her hands about.

Clerk Previous psychiatric treatment?

Edward Child Guidance.

Doctor I A history of erratic behaviour?

Jean Yes.

Doctor II How long has Verity been having treatment for epilepsy?

Edward Three years.

Registrar Name?

Jean Verity Rose Taylor.

Doctor I How long was she missing from home?

Edward Seven hours.

Clerk Age?

Jean Eleven years and five months.

Doctor II Has Verity been in a mental hospital before?

Edward No.

Registrar If you'll just wait here please.

Clerk Right along to the end of the corridor.

Doctor I May I see your doctor's letter?

Doctor II stands. The others stand at once

Doctor II Yes. Well, I think we can admit Verity into our children's ward.

The Doctors, the Clerk and the Registrar pick up their chairs and carry them over to place them deliberately around Verity II like a cage

The Doctors, Clerk and Registrar go off

Edward and Jean move towards Verity II who stands impassive

Jean Good-bye, Verity.

Edward Good-bye. We'll come and see you soon.

Verity II turns her back on them

Jean and Edward look at each other, then go off

The two Veritys are now facing each other

Verity I Dear whoever you are . . .

Verity II (*kneeling and taking up the exact posture of Verity I*) Whoever you are . . .

Black-out

Verity I leaves the stage. Another Edward and Jean come on

Verity II stays in the "cage" silently during the following

Jean A year, Edward! She's been in there a whole year and they still can't tell us what's wrong with her. How can they say she's ready to be discharged when she isn't any better? Is she? Do you think she is? Did you think so today?

Edward I know it was bad today, Jean, but last time we visited her she was quite—placid. They said today was a worse day than usual for her. But you have to expect it sometimes.

Jean Last time! She'd just been having that horrible shock treatment last time. I wouldn't have said placid. Confused. Miles away. Like a strange little old woman. Not like a child. Why did they do that to her? It didn't do any good—no good at all.

Edward Jean, they have to try every kind of treatment they can. She has been better—some of the time. And they think if she comes home now she'll settle down.

Jean Why should she? What makes them think that? Look what happened when they let her come home for Christmas . . .

Jean goes off

Edward (*going to the side of the stage*) But that was six months ago . . .

Verity erupts out from inside the chairs, knocking them over and shouting

Verity II All my presents smell of old socks! Dad! You've been walking all over my Christmas presents with your dirty socks on.

Edward (*coming forward*) Don't be silly, Verity. Of course I haven't.

Verity Doesn't matter. I don't care anyway. I've smashed them all up and thrown them into the dustbin.

Edward Oh Verity . . .

Verity Oh Verity! Oh Verity! I'm the underdog female in this family. I know. I know. That's what you all think I am.

Edward That isn't true. You know that isn't true.

Verity Liar liar pants on fire can't get off the telephone wire. (*She points at him. Fiercely*) She wouldn't take me to the zoo today. She took Mark and Nicky but she wouldn't take me.

Edward (*calmly, sensibly*) That's because you were naughty, Verity. You know perfectly well none of us got any sleep last night. How many times did we tell you if you didn't go to bed quietly and stop all that noise you wouldn't be allowed to go to the zoo.

Verity I wanted to play with Nicky. He liked the music. He likes it loud. He loves it. (*She sings the Ying Tong song loudly and runs round Edward pulling at him*)

Edward He needed to sleep, Verity. We all needed to sleep. (*He gets hold of her and quietens her*) Now then, why don't you start to lay the table for tea? They'll be back soon.

Verity (*with dislike*) Oh yes! Another order! (*Suddenly docile*) All right, Dad.

Edward (*gratefully*) Good girl.

Verity II goes off. Mark comes on

Mark Hello, Dad.

Edward Hello, Mark. Did you have a good time?

Mark Smashing. They've got a new place for nocturnal animals. They use infra-red light. I wish you could've seen it.

Edward Well, we'll go again. Where's your mother?

Mark Putting Nicky to bed. He fell asleep on the way home. (*He looks round. Wary*) Where is she?

Edward Verity? She's in the kitchen.

Jean comes on wearing a cape and scarf

Hello, darling. All right?

Jean Yes. We had a lovely time. Nicky adored it. (*Pause*) How was she?

Edward Not bad. Not bad at all. She was fine.

Jean Thank goodness. I was worried.

Edward She's just gone to set the table for tea.

Jean (*pleased*) Well then.

Verity comes on, her forearms upraised, blood running down them

Verity (*smiling*) Look! Look!
Jean Oh my God!
Edward Verity, what have you done?
Verity (*giggling*) I've carved myself with the carving fork. (*She licks the blood on her arms*) Here's two legs of lamb for tea. Here Mark—do you want some? Have some. Have a bite. Here. (*She goes to Mark pushing her arms at him*)
Mark Get off! Get her off me! (*He rushes over to Jean*) Why are you so stupid? (*He shouts more and more hysterically*) You spoil everything. Go back to the hospital where you belong! Leave us alone!
Jean Ssshhhh—Mark—don't.

Edward grabs hold of Verity and wipes off the blood with his handkerchief

Edward (*very controlled*) They're only scratches. Come along with me, Verity, and we'll put something on them.
Verity (*leaning against him*) All right, Dad.
Edward (*leading her off*) Aren't you a silly girl?
Verity (*breaking violently away from him*) Silly? Silly? I'm not the silly one. I'm not going back to the hospital. (*She rushes over to Jean*) You can go back there. You go. (*She starts pulling at Jean's clothes, yanks the scarf off her neck and puts it round her own. Then she pulls off Jean's cape*)
Mark (*pulling Verity away*) Stop that! Stop doing that to Mum! Leave her alone!
Verity You leave me alone! (*She trips him up and he falls. Then she takes her mother's face in her hands and speaks very gently*) See, Mum? I'll wear your clothes and you can wear mine and then they'll think you're me. (*Again violent, she tears off her own cardigan and throws it in Jean's face*) Have a good time in the hospital, Verity!

Verity runs off

Edward Quick, Mark. Come with me. We must go after her.

Edward hurries off

Mark Let her go. Let her run away and stay away. I don't care.
Jean (*near to tears*) Mark—please.
Mark I'm sorry, Mum. I'm sorry.

Mark goes off in the opposite direction from Edward

Jean picks up Verity's cardigan and folds it. She hugs it to her heart

Jean I can't bear it. I just can't bear it. (*She walks up stage and puts the cardigan down*)

Miss Everitt, a Social Worker, enters down stage

Miss Everitt Mrs Taylor? I'm Miss Everitt, Social Services.
Jean (*going to her and shaking hands*) How do you do. It was good of you to come. Would you like some tea?

Miss Everitt I can't really stay, I'm afraid. I've got three other house visits this afternoon. I don't know whether I'm coming or going this week. I've been making enquiries since I had your husband's letter. (*Pause*) I'm afraid I've got disappointing news for you.

Jean (*flatly*) You can't find a residential place for Verity.

Miss Everitt I'm so sorry. There just doesn't seem to be a suitable boarding school. It's partly her age. Fourteen seems to be too old for most of the schools and then a lot of them just aren't keen to take on someone so—disruptive.

Jean There must be somewhere she could be taken care of. We've tried. We've tried so hard.

Miss Everitt (*business-like*) I'm sure you have.

Jean This last two years has been like a nightmare. She's been back twice to the children's ward at the hospital. Won't they take her in again?

Miss Everitt I've had a letter from them saying in their view she's no longer in need of hospital care. I understand the last two admissions were because of breakdowns. They don't regard the present situation as an emergency, you see.

Jean It is for us!

Miss Everitt (*hastily*) Her headmistress tells me she's doing quite well at school. Holding her own in the c stream.

Jean It's when she's at home. I used to think it must be our fault—that we were doing something wrong. But they couldn't keep her in the Care Home. She was only there three weeks. And in that Rudolf Steiner Centre last month it was only two days.

Miss Everitt Yes. I saw the report. Inciting the other children to destructive behaviour and vandalism.

Jean I don't think that's fair! All she did was get the children to pull down the curtains in the house and put them on as costumes. They went for a fancy dress march in the streets. (*She laughs slightly*) I should think they had a marvellous time.

Miss Everitt (*reprovingly*) That kind of behaviour can't be contained in a Children's Home.

Jean (*angrily*) But it can in our home, can't it! We're supposed to be able to manage without any sleep, without any peace and quiet—frantic and exhausted all the time. I mean all the time, Miss Everitt! She still runs off, you know. The telephone ringing in the middle of the night. The police calling. Again!

Miss Everitt There are much worse cases than Verity, you know, Mrs Taylor. Though of course I can imagine how difficult it is for you.

Jean Can you? I don't think you can. I don't think anyone could. Miss Everitt, we've got a son trying to take A levels. We've got a four-year-old boy. There's no peace in this house for either of them when she's here.

Miss Everett She is your child, Mrs Taylor.

Jean (*passionately*) So are they my children! So are they!

Miss Everitt (*slightly cowed*) Well, we'll certainly continue investigating all the possibilities, Mrs Taylor. But I must warn you that there aren't many facilities for a case like this. We just don't have the places or the staff. We all think you and your husband are managing wonderfully well in the circumstances.

Miss Everitt goes

Jean What are we going to do? Dear God, what are we going to do? Managing! Perhaps it would be better for all of us if we couldn't manage. Then they'd have to do something. Maybe if I became an alcoholic . . . I could. My God, I think I could sometimes. (*Pause*) When I go next door to Suzanne's some nights and we sit and get a bit tight together on the whisky and talk about all sorts of things and laugh—just for a little while I can forget. The thoughts stop going round and round in my head. The relief of just feeling like an ordinary person. The relief. Supposing when Miss Everitt Social Services came round today she'd found me dead drunk on the floor. "Dear me, Mrs Taylor, you're not managing wonderfully well today." (*Pause*) Imagine your own child driving you to drink. Your own child that you love. (*Pause*) I don't even know if I do love her. I don't know what I feel. Pity—oh, pity for her. Why did it have to happen? Poor Verity. Poor, poor baby. (*Pause*) But fear too. She seems to like to frighten me— enjoys it. She never does it to Edward. I really think sometimes she hates me. And he's so good to her—so patient and kind. All those holidays he takes her on. He doesn't talk much about them afterwards but I know, I know she crucifies him. And I feel mean and cowardly because I don't go too. (*Pause*) And guilty. Did I do it? Was it my fault? When I was pregnant with her—all those weeks when she was inside me I thought she was so safe. Nothing could hurt her and yet all the time . . . Was it me? Did I—contaminate her? Oh God . . . (*She stops herself*) She was so beautiful when she was a baby. Even now sometimes when you look at her when she's asleep. When I'm out with her sometimes I wish she was ugly. Deformed or crippled. Something people could *see*. Then they would pity her too. Instead of getting nervous and embarrassed and moving away from us as if we were lepers. Oh God, will nobody help us? Can't anybody help us?

The Lights come up on Edward, writing

Edward Dear Sir, I am writing to you once again to request your help with our acute problems concerning our daughter. It is no exaggeration to say that my wife is quite at the end of her tether after years of trying to give this girl the opportunity of a happy home. I really fear for my wife's health if the situation continues as at present.

Voice I (*out of the darkness*) Dear Mr Taylor, I sympathize with the difficulties you are experiencing with your daughter but must tell you that there are unfortunately no establishments in this area for disturbed teenagers and young adults.

Edward I understand that application has been made to you on behalf of our daughter for a place in your residential unit. I am only writing to underline the urgency of the situation. Our younger son, who is only four, has been suffering acute mental distress in recent months which has been manifested by lack of appetite, sleeplessness and bedwetting. The headmistress of the nursery school that he attends has offered to depose to the effect that his present home situation is having a severe effect on him.

Voice II I am sorry to say that as we run the only adolescent unit within a very large area we are inundated with requests and have no vacant places at present. We will, of course, put your daughter's name on our waiting list.

Edward We can understand the reasons why the Council cannot consider re-admitting Verity into care but I am writing to ask if there is not some kind of "safety net" provided by the council for cases of this sort.

Voice III Although I do ask you to accept that we all sympathize with you in the present situation regarding Verity, there is really nothing that we as the Borough Directorate can do at the present time for you or even advise you to do.

Edward (*standing and looking over to Jean*) Nothing.

Jean I'm leaving home, Edward, and I'm taking Nicky with me.

Black-out. The Lights come up on Verity V sitting C, drawing a circle round herself with her finger

A Staff Member, Dottie, enters and stands by Verity

Dottie Aren't you going to have any breakfast, Verity? It'll all be cold now. Come on with me and I'll make you some hot toast and tea.

Verity looks up at her and silently mouths some words

What? I can't hear you? What did you say?

Verity looks down again and goes on drawing her circle

Tom, the Warden, enters

She won't come and eat her breakfast.

Tom I should leave her. We have to give her time. She's only been here two days. At least she's got out of bed finally. Hello, Verity. You all right in there?

Verity nearly smiles at him and mouths words again. He nods and gives her the thumbs up sign

Dottie I honestly don't think she should have been placed with us, Tom. After all, this is a Half-way House not a mental hospital. It's a bit hard on all the others. We wouldn't let them stay in bed for two days.

Tom Well, Dottie, if this lot can't feel a bit of compassion for her, who can? They know what it's like.

Dottie O.K., Tom, you're the Warden. But I can't help feeling they all want to forget what it was like.

Tom I think there's a chance they may try to help her. Anyway I didn't see how we could refuse. She'd split her family right up, you know. Her mother left home.

Dottie Has she gone back?

Tom nods

Well, that's something. And there certainly hasn't been any violent behaviour. Quite the reverse, really.

Tom Everybody gone off to work?

Dottie Well, everybody but Geoff, Violet and Harry. As usual.

Tom Ah the terrible truants. Let's go and shift them. You'd better hunt up Harry's attaché case. He's bound to have hidden it again.

Dottie (*as they go*) Well, Violet's all yours. She never takes a blind bit of notice of me.

Tom That's because she's a man's woman, you see.

Tom and Dottie laugh, and go

Verity It's exactly around me. It gets smaller and smaller and then it fits me. (*She traces a curved shape above and around herself with her hands*) It's a glass ball. I'm inside it all by myself. When they talk to me I can't hear them inside here. And when I talk they can't hear me. Nobody can touch me. (*Pause. Uncertainly*) I'm a bit afraid in here. (*Rapidly*) No no no it's all right. Make it a bit smaller. (*She scrunches herself up very small and once more traces the circle round herself*)

Tom comes in with Violet, who is a little old lady

Violet (*pleading, frail*) If you could just write them a note, Tom. Tell them I couldn't come in today because my tummy was upset. I'll never be able to fill in those labels if I have an upset tummy.

Tom Upset tummy? After that breakfast? Honestly, Violet, anybody would think you were a farm labourer or something.

Violet (*modestly, pleased*) I always did have a good appetite. My father used to say—(*She sees Verity and waves*) Hello dear.

Verity mouths at her and Violet obligingly mouths back

I think the child's deaf, you know. Perhaps I could learn sign language and then we could . . .

Tom (*warningly*) Violet. Get your hat and coat and get to work.

Violet I feel giddy. I think I'm going to faint.

Tom Well, I'm not going to catch you.

She glares at him. He grins back at her. She smiles

Violet (*cheerfully*) Righto. (*She starts out*)

Harry enters, meeting Violet

(*Reprovingly*) Hurry up, Harry. You'll be late to work.

Violet goes

Harry (*shouting angrily after her*) Well, I can't go to work without my attaché case can I? (*He looks round for it*) Someone's stolen my attaché case.

Dottie enters, holding an attaché case

Dottie It's here, Harry. It was under the hall table.
Harry (*irascibly*) All right, all right, all right. Daft place for it to be.
(*Going toward Dottie, he nearly trips over Verity*) Why don't you look
where's you're going, you stupid girl. (*He takes the case and turns to
Tom. Dolefully*) What's for supper tonight?
Tom Spaghetti.
Harry (*despairingly*) Oh God . . .
Tom And rhubarb crumble.
Harry (*sighing*) I see. (*He nods resignedly*) I see.

Geoff comes in

Harry bumps into him on his way out

For God's sake, Geoff, get out of the way. (*As he goes*) How am I
supposed to get to work on time with everyone trying to knock me
down?

Harry goes

Geoff (*to Dottie, with difficulty*) I'm feeling fairly bad.
Dottie Oh, I'm sorry, Geoff. Perhaps it'll lift a bit when you get to work.
Geoff (*jerkily, stuttering*) Yes—yes—I think—yes—I like it you know—I
—it's a good job—I do—yes. It's just I—it's the streets on the way on
the way on the way. (*He takes a deep breath*) When I'm feeling bad I
get—you know—I feel—I'm afraid a bit a bit a bit . . . (*He stops.
Carefully*) The traffic frightens me.
Dottie Listen, I'll walk along with you to the park. I've got to do the
shopping. That O.K., Tom?
Tom Fine.
Dottie Come on, Geoff. I'll just get the shopping trolley.

Dottie goes

Geoff (*stuttering badly*) G—g—g—g—good-bye,—T—Tom . . .
Tom Bye-bye, Geoff.

Geoff goes

*Tom gets two windowboxes and a bag of bulbs. He sets them down a little
distance from Verity and begins planting the bulbs. She watches. Then, very
slowly, she stands and leaves her circle, takes a step or two toward Tom,
stops, and watches him for a bit*

Verity What are you doing?
Tom (*not looking round*) Planting bulbs in the windowboxes.
Verity (*as if to herself*) I help Suzanne in her garden.

*Although Tom is studiously casual in tone it is clear that he is being extremely
careful*

Tom (*after a pause*) Would you like to help me?

Verity (*quickly*) No.
Tom (*equably*) Okay.

Very gradually she moves closer to him and crouches down at a little distance to watch

Verity What colour will they be?
Tom Well, they're tulips so I expect they'll be red and purple and maybe some of them will be white.

Almost absentmindedly he pushes a little pile of bulbs toward her. Slowly she picks one up and starts to plant it. They work together in silence

What's your favourite colour, Verity?

She does not answer. They continue planting

When we get all these in we'll take the boxes out and put them on the front windowsills. The sun's shining today. And we'll water them. That way they'll get a good start.

Another silence as they work

When it gets a bit warmer it'll be time to plant the seeds. I bought lots of packets the other day.

Another pause while they continue. Tom finishes his box and picks it up. He stands looking down at Verity, who puts the last bulb in her box and sits back on her heels looking at the box

Verity (*peacefully*) Yellow.

He smiles down at her, though she does not see

Tom goes off. Verity picks up her box and follows him

The Lights fade slowly as she goes, then come up on another area of the stage

Edward and Jean come on. Edward has a letter

Jean Let me see the letter. (*She takes it from him and reads*) "Contented". He says, "Verity seems quite contented". (*She smiles at Edward*) He must be a marvellous man, this Tom Barker.
Edward Yes. It really does sound as if it's finally the right place for her. I suppose he is right to say we should leave it another week or so before we visit her.
Jean Well she's only been there a month. And he says she's still not talking to the other people in the house. We must give her time to settle herself in there gradually. Oh Edward, I can hardly believe it. No tantrums, no rages—it's lovely to think of her pottering about helping with the cooking and the cleaning and the garden.
Edward And he actually thinks he may persuade her to take a little part-time job soon.
Jean I hope he won't push her on that. Surely it's enough for now that she feels safe. (*Smiling at him*) Contented.

Edward I'm sure we can trust his judgement. He obviously cares for her. It really does seem as if it's the beginning of the way back for her.
Jean Yes. Thank God. Thank God.

They smile at each other. Black-out. In the darkness each of the five Veritys screams one after another. The Lights come up on Tom with a phone

Tom We don't know whether she jumped or fell, Mr Taylor. We just don't know. It could have been much worse. Her room's on the first floor so it wasn't that far. The legs are all right but I think she's broken most of the bones in her feet. I'm so sorry. I can't tell you how sorry I am. She was fine all day. No different from usual until supper-time. I have no idea what set her off. She just suddenly jumped up and tipped the table over—smashed all the dishes. And then ran upstairs. It all happened so fast. . . . What? . . . Of course, Mr Taylor. Of course I'll take her back, if I possibly can.

The Lights up at once on another area. A Consultant Psychiatrist is there in white coat, with another Edward and Jean

Consultant Impossible.
Jean But Tom Barker's written to us and he says he has a place for her. He's willing to take her back.
Consultant Mrs Taylor, when Verity first went to that Half-way House two years ago she lasted exactly seven weeks. She related only to Barker and that only minimally. Then the sudden total loss of control and the accident.
Jean I know, but . . .
Consultant (*a little impatiently*) We have already tried it once, Mrs Taylor. The trial week-end she spent there last year was a disaster.
Edward You see, Doctor, it's been the only place she's seemed really happy. Couldn't we try it one more time?
Consultant I'm sorry. It's not a gamble we could afford to take again. Verity simply has not got enough stability for that kind of environment. Look at the record, Mr Taylor. At the General Hospital where she was being treated for the broken bones in her feet she attacked one of the nurses. Which is why she was referred to me at this hospital.
Jean Not "attack". She told us she only pushed the nurse away when she . . .
Consultant The report says "severe concussion".
Jean Because she hit her head when she fell! It wasn't Verity's fault that she . . .
Consultant Mrs Taylor, in the seventeen months since Verity was admitted here she has become less and less responsible for her actions, less and less able to manage herself.
Edward Isn't that partly because you've got her in your locked Geriatric Ward? She's only nineteen, for God's sake!
Consultant It's the only ward in this hospital that's been able to contain her, Mr Taylor. Do you think I wanted to put her there? As far as I'm concerned it's a last resort. We've tried everything else. In the last year she's become increasingly disruptive and destructive. She breaks

windows, destroys property, intimidates the other patients and torments
the nurses. And as you know, she has absconded many many times.

Jean Because she's unhappy!

Consultant (*in a matter-of-fact voice*) Yes.

Edward We just feel that a locked ward in a mental hospital is absolutely
the wrong place for her.

Consultant So do I. So do we all, Mr Taylor, but there aren't many right
places for a girl like Verity. I wish to God there were. There has never
been enough money spent on facilities and staff to provide environ-
ments for this kind of case. Let alone research. We don't know how to
help Verity. She's never responded in any sustained way to any kind of
medical treatment or to psychotherapy. No doctor has ever been able
to give a definite diagnosis in her case. She . . .

Jean (*angrily*) Well, locking her up with a lot of crazy old people isn't
the answer!

Consultant The only alternative seems to be that she returns home to
live with you. Shall we arrange that, Mrs Taylor?

Jean (*after a pause*) No.

Edward (*defeatedly*) No.

Black-out. The Lights up on Tom and Violet

Tom No, she's not coming back again, Violet. The Consultant at the
hospital doesn't think it would be wise.

Violet He's right. I'm sorry, Tom, but he is. She upset us. She wouldn't
talk to any of us. Geoff used to run out of the house when she got her
funny turns, poor fellow. And the second time she came here she was
very rude to you, Tom. She was. The language! I don't know what my
father would have thought.

Tom She's learned to talk like that in the hospital, Violet. She's young.
She picked all that up. Like a child does.

Violet We need to be peaceful here, Tom. This place is our home for now.
She frightened us.

Tom I know. Yes, I know.

The Lights fade, then come up on Verity I in the ward, writing in a notebook

Verity I Dear Reader, I am writing my very own play. We are half-way
through now, three scenes to go and then we've made a play, a comedy
play with lots of funny jokes to go on the television. Start our new
comedy series with all your favourite stars. David Bowie to way way
back before I was born. When Nicky was born I had my first nervous
breakdown. First thing that comes here is to get up out of bed at six
in the morning. Wash! Make your own bed! Just do the best you can!
Because God gave his only begotten son. Tell me what music you like
best of T. Rex. Of course I really love David Bowie. A body of gold.
Benny Hill half-way down my brassiere. Oooooh-ha-Benny get off
you're hurting my tit. Please I need them for a beauty contest for Miss
Universe of the century. All right let me feel your puss instead. Oh no,
don't, that's private property. Poo poo plop plop. I'm in the loo during

poo plop plop. Who do you want to have an orgy with? Faster faster
go on write write keep it up. Sausages. Bassoon. I love you terrapin,
terrapin, terrapin. Drunk Wednesday end of January nineteen seventy-
four. (*Singing*) I love you love, my only true love, I love you love love.

*The Lights go down on her as she sings and come up on Verity IV, who
sings the end of the song in unison with her. She is sitting on the edge of the
raised area upstage swinging her legs. She goes on humming the song under
her breath. A few feet away a man and his wife, Ted and Dora, are sitting
in their living-room watching television. Verity is sitting on their garden
wall. During the following she gets up and balances on one foot, waves her
arms, etc. She seems quiet and absorbed*

Dora (*glancing in Verity's direction*) She's still out there.
Ted (*intent on the television*) Well Dora—she's not doing any harm.
Dora But she's been sitting there on our garden wall twenty minutes,
Ted. Perhaps she's lost.
Ted (*glancing out*) She looks old enough to take care of herself. Besides
she seems perfectly happy.

They both gaze at the set

Dora People might think she lives here.

Ted looks at Dora, surprised

Ted So?

Verity begins rhythmically clapping her hands

Dora Well, look at her now. She looks a bit funny to me.
Ted She'll go away if we just ignore her. I want to watch this. I've often
thought of putting up for this programme.
Dora (*with an unkind laugh*) You! Mastermind!
Ted (*defensively*) Now, Dora, how many times have I been able to answer
the questions before they do? (*He stops and listens*) Schopenhauer. (*His
face falls*) Oh. But you must admit that week before last I . . .

Verity begins to perform some kind of gyrating dance on the wall

Dora Ted! Go and speak to her.
Ted (*looking out*) Oh all right. (*He starts to go*) What am I supposed to
say to her?
Dora How do I know? You're the mastermind.

Ted goes "out", regards Verity for a moment, then goes up to her

Ted Uh—hello.
Verity (*smiling briefly at him*) Hello, how are you?
Ted Very well thank you. Uh—do you live near here?
Verity Oh no. Miles away. Miles. I'm lost. (*She hops up and down on the
wall*)
Ted Oh. Well. Perhaps you'd better come in and we'll—uh . . . Look,
come into the house.

Ted moves back into the "house"

Verity Okay. (*She follows him in and sees Dora*) Hello.
Ted She's lost.
Dora Oh that's a shame. Where do you live, dear?
Verity Lots of places. H Twenty-one at the moment.
Ted H Twenty-one?
Verity The ward. I'm glad I'm not in D Two. Sister Moses is the boss
there. She's a shit.
Ted Oh. Ha. Yes. Well.
Verity You've got a nice telly. The one in the ward is tiny. I'm going to
smash it up one night. (*She laughs*)
Dora (*at a loss*) Perhaps you'd like a cup of tea.
Verity No thanks. (*She sits very near the television and watches it intently*)

They watch her, perplexed

(*Casually*) I've just been raped.
Ted What?

Dora, galvanized into action, rises and starts to go out

Dora Would you like a cheese sandwich?
Verity On the M-one. He did it to me in the back of his lorry.
Dora I'm sure you must be hungry—I mean . . . (*She trails off, then goes
on with desperate brightness*) Or ham! A nice ham sandwich!
Verity Then he dragged me on to the verge and he did it to me again. I
didn't like it.

Ted, speechless, just gapes at her

Dora (*extremely briskly*) No I'm sure you didn't, dear. Now I'm just
going to put the kettle on. (*In a tense whisper to Ted*) She's mad! Keep
her talking. I'm going to phone the police. (*Loudly*) Back in a moment.

Dora smiles warmly at Verity and goes off

Verity (*rubbing and clapping her hands, bobbing up and down*) Oh look it's
Star Trek! It's my favourite. (*She looks surprised at Ted, who is still
staring at her*) Aren't you going to watch it?
Ted Uh—yes . . . Yes I am—uh yes. (*Gingerly he sits beside her, keeping
a careful distance*)

The Lights fade on them and come up on the Consultant, sitting

Consultant Dear Mr Taylor, I'm sorry that Verity continues to be a
disappointment to us all. After this last escapade I have been obliged
to place her in D Two, a locked chronic ward for Geriatrics. I am not
happy about this arrangement but there is no other suitable accom-
modation for her in this hospital. You will be relieved to know that the
medical examination showed no signs whatever that she had been
raped. I am afraid we are really at our wits end to know how to help
Verity now.

Sister Moses comes on in another area, followed by four Geriatric Patients dragging chairs and shuffling on

Sister Moses Into the day-room, everyone. Come along!

Verity II comes on and sits on the floor, her back to the others

Sister Moses helps to settle the patients in their chairs. They pay little attention to her

Patient I Don't speak to me. I'll kill you! I'm an assassin for the City of London Police. One hit! Dead!

Patient II Nasty—nasty—nasty . . .

Patient III It ain't gonna rain no more no more it ain't gonna rain no more. (*She drones on with this*)

Patient IV He's a spy! I know. My daughter sent him. Oh I know.

Patient II Dirty—filth—rats in here. I've seen them—dirty.

Patient I Mrs Baker said to me, "Suck my breasts!" One hit! Dead!

Patient IV I want my tea. I want my tea. I want my tea.

Patient III She's wet herself. Silly old cow.

Verity (*her voice strikingly young in comparison*) I want a fag. Hasn't anybody got a fag? Moses! Moses! Got a fag for me, Moses?

Sister Moses (*angrily*) Don't call me Moses—Taylor.

The Physiotherapist comes in, carrying a basket

Here's Miss Blake from Physio. She's going to play some games with you. Up off the floor, please Verity. Off the floor.

Verity gets up and stands sulkily at the side

(*To Miss Blake*) That girl is driving me round the bend. (*To Patient IV*) Oh Elsie, look at you. You've done it again. Why didn't you call me? You know you're supposed to call me when you want the toilet. Come along. Come along.

Sister Moses leads Patient IV off

Miss Blake Well how's everybody today? Jolly good. Shall we have a little ball game first, eh? That's right. We'll just throw the ball back and forth to each other shall we?

Miss Blake gets out a ball and tosses it to two or three of them making encouraging comments, and they more or less manage to get it back to her. Suddenly Verity turns and dashes over, intercepts the ball and runs round bouncing it, pushing it in peoples' faces, rolling it, etc., while she sings loudly

Verity The Mayor of Bayswater, he's got a very pretty daughter and the hair on her dicky dido hangs down to her knees. One black one one white one and one with a bit of shite on and the hair on her dicky dido hangs down to her knees.

Through this Miss Blake tries to get the ball away from her

Sister Moses comes in with Patient IV, sits her down, goes swiftly over to Verity and gets the ball

Sister Moses All right, Verity. That's enough. Out of the day-room. If you can't behave yourself you can't stay in here. Back to the ward.

Verity I won't go back there all by myself. I don't want to! Leave me alone! I wasn't hurting anybody!

Sister Moses (*bundling her towards the door fairly roughly*) Back to the ward I said.

Verity, stamping and scuffing her feet walks over to the raised area and crouches on it

Verity Horrible old Moses. I hate her. I hate this place. I hate this boring place. Boring boring boring!

Miss Blake (*to the Patients*) And now a few exercises I think. One leg out, everyone. Now rotate the foot from the ankle. (*She demonstrates. Some of them more or less follow suit*) Good. Good. Jolly good. Now the other one.

Verity I'll get her. (*She jumps up*) I know what I'll do. (*She scrambles off the raised area*)

Verity goes off

Miss Blake Arms above heads now. Right up. Up up up. That's right. Now round and round with the hands. Nice and loose. Now shake the hands. Shake shake shake.

Verity comes back up with a wastepaper-basket

Verity She doesn't know I hid these under my mattress. (*She shakes a box of matches*) I'll show her.

Laughing, Verity strikes match after match and drops them into the basket.

A red light comes up on her

Miss Blake And now we'll just relax our necks shall we? Eyes closed, everyone, and drop the head forward on to the chest and now take the head round very slowly . . . (*She goes from one Patient to the other, helping them, talking to them*)

Verity I'll get her chair. I'll get Sister Mose's chair. (*She scrambles off and grabs it up. Puts it over the basket*) When she sits down it'll burn her backside. It'll burn her ass off! (*She laughs*)

Sister Moses I smell smoke! Something's burning!

The red Light on Verity goes out. The Patients rise and stand by their chairs

The Consultant enters

Patient I walks across to meet him. Miss Blake takes Patient I's chair and puts it C, facing out. Verity comes and stands behind it, as if in a witness-box

Patient I (now Edward) You've said again and again she's not responsible for her actions. And now she's to be prosecuted for six pounds worth of damage to a wooden chair?

Consultant The fire service are called to the hospital by law when there is any kind of fire no matter how small. The police arrived with them. They made enquiries to know whether in my opinion Verity was of a fit frame of mind to know what she was doing and I have no doubt that this was so.

Patient II moves a chair to below Verity II, facing out, then stands upstage. Sister Moses walks downstage and joins Edward

Sister Moses (now Jean) Holloway! They can't be going to put her in Holloway, Edward.

Patient IV Verity Taylor has been under my care as Medical Officer since her reception at Holloway. From reviewing her history, seeing her parents and from my own observations I believe she is a severely disturbed girl. Although I do not regard her as a dangerous patient, there is no doubt that she responds well to a firm, understanding, contained and consistent environment. Ordinary mental hospitals are unable to contain or help her. (*She moves her chair to place it at the side of Verity, facing out*)

Edward (*to Jean*) She's been committed to a hearing at Canterbury Crown Court.

Jean What will happen to her? What will happen to her now?

Consultant Ideally what she needs is a maximum security institution where she cannot abscond, where there are sufficient nurses to give her individual attention and where there is some form of psychotherapeutic programme which would help her to undergo a behavioural modification. Unfortunately, the only institution that would provide this is Broadmoor. (*He moves a chair to make the fourth side of the square round Verity II*)

Patient II As a Consultant Psychiatrist for Broadmoor Hospital it is my opinion that she must be contained for a prolonged period of treatment in conditions of security. In view of her long history and in order to provide statutory supervision as well as a hospital order I suggest that under Section sixty-five of the Mental Health Act a restriction order without limit of time be put upon her discharge from hospital.

All the Lights go out, except for Verity II in her cage of chairs

The other four Veritys come and sit in the chairs

Narrator (*out of the darkness*) In November nineteen seventy-five at the age of twenty, Verity Taylor was charged by the police with the damage of a chair by fire, value six pounds, in a locked ward of a mental hospital where she was a patient. She was remanded in custody to Holloway Prison for a period of three months. She was subsequently tried at Canterbury Crown Court and in February nineteen seventy-six an order was made for her admission to a maximum security hospital. On February the twenty-fourth, nineteen seventy-six, Verity Taylor

was admitted to Broadmoor from where she may not be transferred
elsewhere without the permission of the Home Secretary.

All Five Veritys (*to the audience, one after another, loudly*) Find me!

Black-out

the CURTAIN *falls*

FURNITURE AND PROPERTY LIST

If desired, the play can be produced without props (see Production Note, page v):
a list of main props mentioned in the action, together with essential furniture, is
given below. All can be brought on and off by various characters

Several upright wooden chairs
2 small tables
Television set

Set of child's blocks **(Verity)**
School report **(Teacher)**
Umbrella **(Jean)**
Newspaper **(Mother I)**
Umbrella **(Mother II)**
Pencils **(Schoolchildren)**
Menus, crockery, cutlery, plates of food, napkins, trays **(French Family, Waitress)**
Money **(Edward)**
Wine bottle, Coca Cola, glasses **(Edward, Children)**
Notebook, pencil **(Admissions Clerk)**
2 letters **(Edward)**
Pen, paper **(Edward)**
Attaché case **(Dottie)**
2 windowboxes, 2 small trowels, bag of bulbs **(Tom)**
Telephone **(Tom)**
Notebook, pencil **(Verity)**
Basket **(Physiotherapist)**
Ball **(Miss Blake)**
Wastepaper-basket **(Verity)**
Matches **(Verity)**

LIGHTING PLOT

Property fittings required: nil
A bare stage

To open: Black-out

Cue 1	As action starts *Bring up lighting on raised area*	**(Page 1)**
Cue 2	**Verity V:** "Find me." *Bring up lighting on Verity II*	**(Page 1)**
Cue 3	**Verity II:** "Find me." *Cross-fade to Interviewer*	**(Page 2)**
Cue 4	As **Verity III** enters *Cross-fade to Verity III*	**(Page 3)**
Cue 5	**Edward** and **Jean** go off *Cross-fade to Teacher*	**(Page 5)**
Cue 6	**Teacher:** "Come along, Class Two. Hurry up." *Cross-fade to downstage area*	**(Page 6)**
Cue 7	**Mother II:** ". . . flu about, isn't there?": **Jean:** "Yes." *Cross-fade to Teacher*	**(Page 6)**
Cue 8	**Jean** exits *Cross-fade to Mark*	**(Page 8)**
Cue 9	**Jean, Edward, Verity** and **Mark** exit *Bring up lighting on restaurant area*	**(Page 9)**
Cue 10	**Neighbour I:** "Go on, Verity." *Slow fade to glow on Verity*	(Page 12)
Cue 11	**Neighbours:** "Light the fire! Light the fire!" *Red flicker on bonfire*	(Page 13)
Cue 12	**Verity** "freezes" with arms up *Fade red flicker, cross-fade to swimming-pool area*	(Page 13)
Cue 13	**Verity V:** "Verity Taylor the winner!" *Black-out*	(Page 14)
Cue 14	**Verity:** "No! No! No!" *Bring up spot on Verity*	(Page 14)
Cue 15	**Verity** (*rushing off*): "Neetz! Neetz! Neetz!" *Black-out*	(Page 15)
Cue 16	**Verity:** "Get out of my way!" *Bring up spot on Verity*	(Page 15)

Cue 17	After **Verity's** exit (or after Optional Interval) *Bring up lighting on raised area and downstage*	(Page 16)
Cue 18	**Verity II:** "Whoever you are . . ." *Black-out, then lighting up on Edward, Jean and Verity in cage*	(Page 20)
Cue 19	**Jean:** "I just can't bear it." *Concentrate lighting on Jean and Miss Everitt*	(Page 22)
Cue 20	**Miss Everitt** goes *Fade to spot on Jean*	(Page 24)
Cue 21	**Jean:** "Can't anybody help us?" *Bring up spot on Edward*	(Page 24)
Cue 22	**Jean:** ". . . taking Nicky with me." *Black-out, then bring up lighting on Verity V and surrounding area*	(Page 25)
Cue 23	**Verity** exits with bulbs *Slow cross-fade to Edward and Jean*	(Page 28)
Cue 24	**Jean** and **Edward** smile at each other *Black-out*	(Page 29)
Cue 25	After the five **Veritys** scream *Bring up spot on Tom*	(Page 29)
Cue 26	**Tom:** ". . . if I possibly can." *Cross-fade to Consultant Psychiatrist, Edward and Jean*	(Page 29)
Cue 27	**Jean:** "No.": **Edward:** "No." *Black-out then bring up lighting on Tom and Violet*	(Page 30)
Cue 28	**Tom:** "I know. Yes, I know." *Cross-fade to Verity*	(Page 30)
Cue 29	**Verity:** "I love you love love." *Cross-fade to Verity IV and television area*	(Page 31)
Cue 30	**Ted** sits beside **Verity** *Cross-fade to Consultant*	(Page 32)
Cue 31	**Consultant:** ". . . to help Verity now." *Cross-fade to day-room area*	(Page 32)
Cue 32	As **Verity** strikes matches *Bring up red spot on Verity*	(Page 34)
Cue 33	**Sister Moses:** "Something's burning!" *Fade red spot*	(Page 34)
Cue 34	**Patient II:** ". . . upon her discharge from hospital." *Fade all lighting except for Verity II in her cage of chairs*	(Page 35)
Cue 35	**All Five Veritys** (*in succession*): "Find me!" *Black-out*	(Page 36)

EFFECTS PLOT

Cue 1	Red spot flickers on bonfire *Sound of rockets and fireworks*	(Page 13)
Cue 2	**Verity** exits shouting "Neetz! Neetz! Neetz!" *Banging and thumping sounds*	(Page 15)
Cue 3	**Edward:** ". . . locked herself in the bathroom." *Sound of pounding on door*	(Page 15)
Cue 4	**Edward:** "Verity, come out! Come out!" *Sound of rushing water*	(Page 15)

Printed in the United Kingdom by
Hobbs the Printers Ltd, Totton, Hampshire SO40 3WX

MUSIC USE NOTE

Licensees are solely responsible for obtaining formal written permission from copyright owners to use copyrighted music in the performance of this play and are strongly cautioned to do so. If no such permission is obtained by the licensee, then the licensee must use only original music that the licensee owns and controls. Licensees are solely responsible and liable for all music clearances and shall indemnify the copyright owners of the play(s) and their licensing agent, Samuel French, against any costs, expenses, losses and liabilities arising from the use of music by licensees. Please contact the appropriate music licensing authority in your territory for the rights to any incidental music.

IMPORTANT BILLING AND CREDIT REQUIREMENTS

If you have obtained performance rights to this title, please refer to your licensing agreement for important billing and credit requirements.